THE T

and Other Stories

Thomas Hardy is probably best known for his novels such as *Tess of the d'Urbervilles*, but he also wrote a great number of short stories. Many of them were based on stories told by people in the villages around where he lived in the south of England.

People are the same, whether they live in the town or the country, today or a hundred years ago. From his hut a young shepherd boy watches, wide-eyed and afraid, a secret meeting between a woman and a man who is not her husband. A young teacher, going home to marry a much older man, has a moment of madness that will change her life.

But we begin with a knock on the door at a lonely cottage. Inside, all is bright and cheerful, with music and dancing, and people enjoying themselves. Outside, the rain beats down, and the stranger following the footpath across the wild hills stares at the lighted windows. Should he go on, or can he stop for a while, to find rest and food and a seat by a warm fire?

OXFORD BOOKWORMS LIBRARY
Classics

The Three Strangers
and Other Stories

Stage 3 (1000 headwords)

Series Editor: Jennifer Bassett
Founder Editor: Tricia Hedge
Activities Editors: Jennifer Bassett and Christine Lindop

THOMAS HARDY

The Three Strangers

and Other Stories

Retold by
Clare West

Illustrated by
Adam Stower

OXFORD UNIVERSITY PRESS

OXFORD
UNIVERSITY PRESS

Great Clarendon Street, Oxford OX2 6DP

Oxford University Press is a department of the University of Oxford.
It furthers the University's objective of excellence in research, scholarship,
and education by publishing worldwide in

Oxford New York

Auckland Cape Town Dar es Salaam Hong Kong Karachi
Kuala Lumpur Madrid Melbourne Mexico City Nairobi
New Delhi Shanghai Taipei Toronto

With offices in

Argentina Austria Brazil Chile Czech Republic France Greece
Guatemala Hungary Italy Japan Poland Portugal Singapore
South Korea Switzerland Thailand Turkey Ukraine Vietnam

OXFORD and OXFORD ENGLISH are registered trade marks of
Oxford University Press in the UK and in certain other countries

This simplified edition © Oxford University Press 2008

Database right Oxford University Press (maker)

First published in Oxford Bookworms 2003

The story entitled *A Moment of Madness* was published in its
original version under the title *A Mere Interlude*

2 4 6 8 10 9 7 5 3

ISBN 978 0 19 479133 5

Printed in Hong Kong

Word count (main text): 11,680 words

For more information on the Oxford Bookworms Library,
visit www.oup.com/bookworms

CONTENTS

The Three Strangers

1
The first stranger

In the south-west of England there are many long, low, grassy hills, which have not changed their appearance for centuries. Farmers still keep their sheep on them, and the only buildings are lonely cottages, where shepherds live.

Fifty years ago there was a shepherd's cottage on one of these hills. It was only three miles from the market town of Casterbridge, but it was unusual for travellers to pass this way. There was no road, just two footpaths which crossed in front of the cottage door. During the long winters, snow and rain fell heavily here, which made travelling difficult.

The night of March 28th, 1825, was one of the coldest and wettest that winter, but inside the cottage all was warm and cheerful. Shepherd Fennel had invited family and friends to drink to the health of his youngest child, a recent arrival in the family. Nineteen people were at the party: married women and single girls, shepherds and farm workers, young people talking of love, and old friends talking of the past.

Shepherd Fennel had chosen his wife well. She was a farmer's daughter from one of the valleys, and when she married, she brought fifty pounds with her in her pocket – and kept it there, for the needs of a coming family. She did not like to spend money unnecessarily, and had worried about the

1

kind of party to give that evening. 'At a sit-still party,' she thought, 'the men'll get too comfortable and drink the house dry. But at a dancing-party people get hungry and then they'll eat all our food! We'll have both sitting *and* dancing – that's the best way.' And secretly she told the fiddler to play for no more than fifteen minutes at a time.

But when the dancing began, nobody wanted to stop. The fiddler refused to catch Mrs Fennel's eye, and played on. The music got louder and louder, and the excited dancers stepped faster and faster. Mrs Fennel could do nothing about it, so she sat helplessly in a corner, as the minutes became an hour.

While this was happening indoors, outside in the heavy rain and darkness a figure was climbing up the hill from Casterbridge. It was a tall, thin man, about forty years old, dressed all in black and wearing thick, heavy boots.

When he reached the shepherd's cottage, the rain came down harder than ever. The man left the footpath and went up to the door. He listened carefully, but the music inside had now stopped, and the man seemed unsure what to do. He looked around, but could see no one on the footpath behind him, and no other houses anywhere near.

At last he decided to knock on the door.

'Come in!' called Shepherd Fennel. All eyes turned towards the stranger, as he entered the warm room.

He kept his hat on, low over his face. 'The rain is heavy, friends,' he said in a rich, deep voice. 'May I come in and rest here for a while?'

'O' course, stranger,' replied the shepherd. 'You've

chosen your moment well, because we're having a party tonight. There's a new baby in the family, you see.'

'I hope you and your fine wife'll have many more, shepherd,' the man answered, smiling politely at Mrs Fennel. He looked quickly round the room, and seemed happy with what he saw. He took his hat off, and shook the water from his shoulders.

'Will you have a drink with us, stranger?' asked Fennel. He passed a mug of his wife's home-made mead to the newcomer, who drank deeply from it and held it out for more.

'I'll take a seat in the chimney corner, if you don't mind,' said the man, 'to dry my clothes a bit.' He moved closer to the fire, and began to look very much at home.

'There's only one more thing that I need to make me happy,' he added, 'and that's a little tobacco.'

'I'll fill your pipe,' said the shepherd kindly.

'Can you lend me one?'

'You're a smoker, and you've no pipe?' said Fennel.

'I dropped it somewhere on the road.' The man lit the pipe that Fennel gave him, and seemed to want to talk no more.

2
The second stranger

During this conversation the other visitors had not taken much notice of the stranger, because they were discussing what the fiddler should play next. They were just getting up to start another dance when there was a second knock at the

3

door. At this sound, the stranger turned his back to the door, and seemed very busy trying to light his pipe.

'Come in!' called Shepherd Fennel a second time. In a moment another man entered. He too was a stranger.

This one was very different from the first. There was a more cheerful look about him. He was several years older, with greying hair and a full, reddish face. Under his long wet coat he was wearing a dark grey suit.

'I must ask to rest here for a few minutes, friends,' he said, 'or I shall be wet to the skin before I reach Casterbridge.'

'Make yourself at home, sir,' replied Fennel, a little less warmly than when welcoming the first stranger. The cottage was not large, there were not many chairs, and these newcomers brought cold, wet air into the room.

The second visitor took off his coat and hat, and sat down heavily at the table, which the dancers had pushed into the chimney corner. He found himself sitting next to the first stranger, who smiled politely at him and passed him the mug of mead. The second man took it, lifted it to his mouth, and drank without stopping, watched by Mrs Fennel, who was not pleased at this free drinking of her best mead.

At last the man in the grey suit put down the mug with a happy sigh. 'That's wonderful mead, shepherd!' he said. 'I haven't tasted anything as good as that for many years.'

'I'm pleased you enjoy it, sir!' replied Shepherd Fennel.

'It's goodish mead,' agreed his wife, a little coldly. 'Made from our own honey, o' course, and it is trouble enough to make, I can tell ye. But we may not make any more – honey

4

sells well, and we don't need much mead for ourselves.'

'Oh, but you can't stop making this!' cried the man in grey. He took the mug again and drank the last drop. 'I love mead, as much as I love going to church on Sundays, or giving money to the poor!'

'That's wonderful mead!' said the man in the grey suit.

a long time ago = before long

'Ha, ha, ha!' said the man by the fire, who seemed to enjoy the stranger's little joke.

The old mead of those days, made with the best honey and the freshest eggs, tasted very strong, but it did not taste as strong as it actually was. Before long, the stranger in grey became very cheerful and red in the face. He made himself comfortable in his chair, and continued the conversation.

'Well, as I say, I'm on my way to Casterbridge,' he said.

'You don't live there then?' said Shepherd Fennel.

'Not yet, although I plan to move there soon.'

'Going to start a business, perhaps?' asked the shepherd.

'No, no,' said his wife. 'It is easy to see that the gentleman is rich, and doesn't need to work at anything.'

'Rich is not the word for me, madam,' replied the man in grey. 'I have to work, and I do work. And even if I only get to Casterbridge by midnight tonight, I must begin work there at eight o'clock tomorrow morning. Yes, hot or cold, rain or snow, I must do my day's work tomorrow.'

'Poor man! So, although you look rich and comfortable, your life is harder than ours, is it?' said the shepherd's wife.

'Well, it's the work that I have to do, that's all. Now I must leave you, friends. But before I go, there's time for one more drink to your baby's health. Only, the mug is empty.'

'Here's some small mead, sir,' offered Mrs Fennel. 'We call it small, but it's still made from good honey.'

'No,' said the stranger. 'I prefer to remember the taste of your best mead, thank you.'

'Of course you do,' said Shepherd Fennel quickly. He went

to the dark place under the stairs where the best mead was kept, and filled the mug. His wife followed him and spoke worriedly to him in a low voice.

'I don't like the look o' the man at all! He's drunk enough for ten men already! Don't give him any more o' the best!'

'But he's in our house, my love, and 'tis a miserable wet night. What's a mug of mead more or less?'

'Very well, just this time then,' she said, looking sadly at the mead. 'But who is he, and what kind of work does he do?'

'I don't know. I'll ask him again.'

While the man in grey drank his mead, Fennel asked him again about his work, but the man did not reply at once. Suddenly the first stranger spoke from his seat by the fire.

'Anybody may know what *I* do – I work with wheels.'

'And anybody may know what *I* do,' said the man in the grey suit, 'if they're clever enough to find it out.'

There was a short silence, which the shepherd's wife broke by calling for a song. The second mug of mead had made the stranger's face even redder and more cheerful than before, and he offered to sing the first song. This is what he sang:

> *My job is the strangest one,*
> *Honest shepherds all —*
> *Work that all the world can see;*
> *My customers I tie, and I take them up so high,*
> *And send 'em to a far country!*

No one spoke, except the man near the fire, who joined in the last part, with a deep, musical voice:

> *And send 'em to a far country!*

7

None of the people in the room understood what the singer meant, except the man near the fire, who continued smoking, and said calmly, 'Go on, stranger! Sing on!'

The man in grey drank again from his mug, and sang:

> *There isn't much I need,*
> *Honest shepherds all —*
> *To set the criminals free.*
> *A little piece of rope, and a tall hanging post,*
> *And that'll be enough for me!*

Now it was clear to everybody in the room that the stranger was answering the shepherd's question in song. They all looked at him, their eyes and mouths wide open in horror.

Everyone looked at the stranger, their eyes and mouths wide open in horror.

8

'Oh, he's the hangman!' they whispered to each other.
'He's come to hang that poor clockmaker tomorrow in
Casterbridge prison – the clockmaker who had no work, and
whose children had no food, so he stole a sheep, and now he's
going to hang for it!'

3
The third stranger

Just then, there was another knock on the door. People
seemed frightened, and Shepherd Fennel was slow to call out,
for the third time, the welcoming words, 'Come in!'

The door was gently opened, and another stranger stood
in the doorway. He was a little man, with fair hair, and was
tidily dressed. 'Can you tell me the way to—?' he began, but
stopped speaking when his eyes fell on the stranger in grey,
who, at that moment, started singing again.

> *Tomorrow is my working day,*
> *Honest shepherds all —*
> *Working with the little piece of rope.*
> *A sheep has lost its life, and the thief must pay the price.*
> *He'll find some peace with God, we hope!*

The man by the fire repeated cheerfully in his deep voice:
> *He'll find some peace with God, we hope!*

All this time the third stranger had stood in the doorway,
and now everyone turned to look at him. They saw to their
surprise that his face was white, his hands were shaking, and
his eyes were fixed in horror on the man in grey. A moment

9

later he turned, and ran away into the darkness and the rain.

'Who can that be?' asked Shepherd Fennel.

No one answered. The room was silent, although there were more than twenty people in it, and nothing could be heard except the rain beating on the windows.

The stillness was broken by a bang. It was the sound of a gun, and it came from Casterbridge.

The third stranger ran away into the darkness and the rain.

'What does that mean?' cried several people at once.

'A prisoner's escaped from Casterbridge prison – that's what it means,' replied the man in grey, jumping up from his chair. 'I wonder if it's *my* man?'

'It must be!' said the shepherd. 'And I think we've seen him! The little man who looked in at the door just now, and shook like a leaf when he saw ye and heard your song!'

'His face was as white as a sheet,' said the fiddler.

'His hands shook like an old man's,' said a farm worker.

'His heart seemed as heavy as a stone,' said Mrs Fennel.

'True,' said the man by the fire. 'His face was white, his hands shook, and he ran like the wind – it's all true.'

'We were all wondering what made him run off like that,' said one of the women, 'and now 'tis explained.'

'Is there a policeman here?' asked the hangman.

One of the men came slowly forward, pushed by his friends. 'I'm one o' the king's officers, sir,' he said.

'Then take some of these men at once, follow the criminal, and bring him back here. He hasn't gone far, I'm sure.'

'I will, sir, I will, when I've got my uniform. I'll go home and put it on, and come back here immediately!'

'Uniform! Never mind about your uniform! The man'll be far away by that time!'

'But I must have my uniform! There's the king's name on it in gold – I can't arrest a man without my uniform on.'

'I'm a king's man myself,' said the man in grey coldly, 'and I order you to find and arrest this man at once! Now then, all the men in the house must come with us. Are you ready?'

11

The men left the cottage to start their search, and the women ran upstairs to see the new baby, who had begun to cry loudly. But the living room did not stay empty for long. A few minutes later the first stranger came quietly back into the house. He cut himself a large piece of cake, and drank another mug of mead. He was still eating when another man came in just as quietly. It was the man in grey.

'Oh, you here?' said the hangman, smiling. 'I thought you had gone to help look for the prisoner.'

'And I thought you had gone too,' replied the other.

'Well, I felt that there were enough people without me,' said the man in grey, helping himself to the mead.

'I felt the same as you.'

'These shepherd-people can easily find the man because they know this hilly country. They'll have him ready for me by the morning, and it'll be no trouble to me at all.'

'Yes, they'll find him. We'll save ourselves all that trouble.'

'True, true. Well, I'm going to Casterbridge. Are you going the same way? We could walk together.'

'No, I'm sorry to say I'm going the other way.' And after finishing their mead, the two men shook hands warmly, said goodbye to each other, and went their different ways.

Out on the hills, the shepherd and his friends were getting cold and wet in their search for the prisoner. They had no luck at all until they reached the top of a hill, where a single tree stood. Suddenly they saw the man who they were looking for, standing next to the tree.

'Your money or your life!' cried the policeman loudly.

Suddenly they saw the man they were looking for.

'No, no,' whispered the shepherd. 'That's what robbers say, not good, honest people like us!'

'Well, I must say something, mustn't I? Ye don't realize how difficult it is to remember what to say!'

The little man now seemed to notice them for the first time. 'Well, travellers, did I hear ye speak to me?' he asked.

'You did,' replied the policeman. 'We arrest ye for not waiting in Casterbridge prison for your hanging tomorrow!'

The little man did not seem at all afraid, and to everyone's surprise agreed with great politeness to go back to the shepherd's cottage. When they arrived there, they discovered that two officers from Casterbridge prison, and a judge who lived nearby, were waiting for them.

'Gentlemen,' said the policeman, 'I've brought back your prisoner – here he is!'

'But this is not our man!' cried one of the prison officers.

'What?' said the judge. 'Haven't you got the right man?'

'But then who can this man be?' asked the policeman.

'I don't know,' said the prison officer. 'But our prisoner is very different. He's tall and thin, with a deep, musical voice.'

'That was the stranger who sat by the fire!' cried Fennel.

The little man now spoke to the judge for the first time. 'Sir,' he said, 'I must explain. I've done nothing wrong – my only crime is that the prisoner is my brother. Today I was on my way to visit him in Casterbridge prison for the last time, when I got lost in the dark. I stopped here to ask the way, and when I opened the door, I saw my brother sitting by the fire. Right next to him was the hangman who'd come to take his

suppose

life! My brother looked at me, and I knew he meant, "Don't tell them who I am, or I'll die!" I was too frightened to do anything except turn and run away.'

'And do you know where your brother is now?'

'No, sir. I haven't seen him since I left the cottage.'

'And what's his job?'

'He's a clockmaker, sir.'

'He said he worked with wheels,' said Shepherd Fennel. 'He meant the wheels of clocks and watches, I suppose.'

'Well, we must let this poor man go,' said the judge. 'Clearly, it's his brother who is the wanted man.'

And so the little man left the cottage with a sad, slow step.

The next morning, men were out on the hills again, searching for the clever thief. But the shepherds and farm workers did not look very carefully. They did not think the man should hang, just for stealing a sheep, and they liked the wonderful coolness that he showed, when sitting next to the hangman at the shepherd's party. So the prisoner was never found, and the man in grey never did his morning's work in Casterbridge, nor ever met again the friendly stranger who had sung the hangman's song with him by the shepherd's fire.

گور

The grass has long been green on the graves of Shepherd Fennel and his wife, and the baby whose health was drunk that night is now an old lady. But the arrival of the three strangers at the shepherd's cottage, and all that happened afterwards, is a story as well known as ever in the hills and valleys around Casterbridge.

15

executed

What the Shepherd Saw

A Story of Four Moonlight Nights

1

First night

The Christmas moon was showing her cold face to the low hills called the Marlbury Downs, in the south-western part of England known as Mid-Wessex. Here sheep were kept out on the hills all year round, and lambs were born as early as December. Shepherds needed to be on the hills day and night at this time of year, and often used small wheeled huts where they could rest and keep warm, while keeping a careful eye on the sheep.

On a high piece of land one of these huts stood inside a little circle of trees, which kept it out of the icy wind and also hidden from any passers-by. The hut was made of wood, and had a door and two windows. The north one looked out on the eight hundred sheep which were in the shepherd's care, and the south window gave a view of three ancient stones, built in the shape of a doorway. These great stones, which village people called the Devil's Door, had been there for over two thousand years. They were worn and weather-beaten, but tonight looked almost new in the silver light of the moon.

Inside the hut a young shepherd boy was waiting for his master, who entered at that moment.

'Are ye sleepy?' asked the old man crossly.

'N–no, master,' replied the boy, who was a little frightened of the shepherd and his heavy stick.

'The sheep should be all right until the morning now,' said the shepherd, 'but one of us must stay here, so I'll leave ye, do ye hear? I'll go home and sleep for a few hours. Run down to my cottage and fetch me if anything happens. Ye can have a bit of a sleep in the chair by the stove – but only for a few minutes, mind! Make sure ye stay awake the rest of the time, and don't let that fire go out!' .

The old man closed the door, and disappeared. The boy went out to check on the sheep and new-born lambs, then came back into the hut and sat down by the warm stove. Soon his eyes closed, his head dropped, and he was asleep.

When he woke up, he could hear down in the valley the clock at Shakeforest Towers striking eleven. The sound carried well in the cold night air. He looked out of the north window and saw the sheep, lying on the grass as quietly as before. He next looked out of the opposite window, towards the stones of the Devil's Door, white and ghostly in the moonlight. And in front of them stood a man.

It was clear that he was not a farm worker, because he was wearing a dark suit, and carried himself like a gentleman. The boy was still wondering, in great surprise, why the man was visiting the Devil's Door at this hour, when suddenly another figure appeared. This second figure was a woman, and when the stranger saw her, he hurried towards her. He met her near the trees, and took her into his arms.

'You have come, Harriet! Thank you!' he cried warmly.

'But not for this,' replied the lady, pulling away from him. She added more kindly, 'I have come, Fred, because you begged me! Why did you ask to see me?'

'Harriet, I have seen many lands and faces since I last walked these hills, but I have only thought of you.'

'Was it only to tell me this that you begged me to meet you, out here on the hills, so late at night?'

'Harriet, be honest with me! I have heard that the Duke is unkind to you.'

'Why did you ask to see me?' Harriet said.

'He sometimes gets angry, but he is a good husband.'

'Harriet, dearest, is that really true? Doesn't everybody know that your life with him is a sad one? I have come to find out what I can do. You are a Duchess, and I'm only Fred Ogbourne, but it's still possible that I can help you. By God! The sweetness of your voice should keep him pleasant, especially when the sweetness of your face is added to it!'

'Captain Ogbourne!' she cried, half afraid, half playful. 'You're an old friend – how can you speak to me in this way? Remember I'm a married woman! I was wrong to come, I see that now.'

'You call me Captain Ogbourne,' he replied unhappily, 'but I was always Fred to you before. I think you no longer have any feeling for me. My love for you, Harriet, has not changed at all, but you are a different woman now. I must accept it. I can never see you again.'

'You needn't talk like that, you stupid man. You can see me again – why not? But of course, not like this. It was a mistake of mine to come tonight, and I only did it because the Duke is away at the moment.'

'When does he return?'

'The day after tomorrow, or the day after that.'

'Then meet me again tomorrow night.'

'No, Fred, I cannot.'

'If you cannot tomorrow night, you can the night after. Please let me have *one* more meeting before he returns, to say goodbye! Now, promise me!' He took the Duchess's hand.

'No, Fred, let go of my hand! It's not kind of you to make

me feel sorry for you, and then to keep me here like this!'

'But see me once more! I have come two thousand miles to see you.'

'Oh, I must not! People will talk. Don't ask it of me!'

'Then confess two things to me; that you did love me once, and that your husband is unkind to you often enough to make you think of the time when you loved me.'

'Yes, I confess them both,' she answered quietly.

'Come once more!' He still held her hand, and had his arm around her waist.

'Very well, then,' she said finally. 'I agree. I'll meet you tomorrow night or the night after. Now let me go.'

He set her free, and watched her hurry down the hill towards her home, Shakeforest Towers. Then he turned and walked away. In a few minutes all was silent and empty again.

But only for a moment. Suddenly, a third figure appeared, from behind the stones. He was a man of heavier build than the Captain, and was wearing riding boots. It was clear that he had watched the meeting between the Captain and the Duchess. He had been too far away to hear their conversation and the lady's reluctant words, so to him they had the appearance of lovers. But several more years passed before the boy was old enough to understand this.

This third figure stood still for a moment, thinking. Then he went back into the trees, and came out again with his horse. He rode off, and the sound of the horse's feet on the hard ground was heard for several minutes, until it died away.

The boy stayed in the hut, his eyes still on the stones, but

Suddenly, a third figure appeared, from behind the stones.

nobody else appeared there. Suddenly he felt a heavy hand on his shoulder, which made him jump.

'Now look here, young Bill Mills, ye've let the fire in the stove go out! Well, what's happened, ye bad boy?'

'Nothing, master.'

'Sheep and lambs all safe and well?'

'Yes, master.'

The old shepherd spoke angrily. 'Well, that's where ye're wrong. There are two new lambs out there, born just this minute, and one of the mothers is half dead! I told ye to stay

21

awake, boy, and fetch me if I was needed! Well, what have you got to say for yourself?'

'You said that I could have a bit of a sleep! In the chair by the stove, you said!'

'Don't you speak to your elders and betters like that, young man, or you'll end up hanging from a rope at the prison! Well, ye can go home now, and come back again by breakfast time. I'm an old man, but there's no rest for me!'

The old shepherd then lay down inside the hut, and the boy went down the hill to his home in the village.

2
Second night

The next evening the old shepherd left the boy alone in the hut again, with repeated orders to keep a careful eye on the sheep. But young Bill was only interested in the view from the south window. He watched and waited, while the moonlight shone on the ancient stones, but neither Captain nor Duchess appeared.

When he heard the Shakeforest Towers clock strike eleven, he saw the third figure appear. As the man came towards the hut, the moonlight shone full on his face, and the boy realized in horror that it was the Duke. All the villagers lived in fear of the Duke. He owned every farm and every house for miles around, and anybody who made him angry could lose their home and their job in a moment. The boy closed the stove, and quickly hid himself in a corner of the hut.

22

The Duke came close to the place where his wife and the Captain had stood the night before. He looked around, perhaps for a hiding-place. When he discovered the hut among the trees, he entered, and stood at the south window, looking out at the Devil's Door.

Only a minute or two later the Captain arrived, to wait for the Duchess. But a terrible surprise was waiting for him tonight, as well as for the frightened boy hidden in the hut. At the Captain's appearance, the Duke became very angry. He opened the door of the hut and stepped out.

'You have dishonoured her, and for that you shall die!' he cried. In the hut, the boy left his hiding-place and ran to the window. He could not see the two men, but he heard something falling on the grass, and then silence.

Three minutes later he saw the Duke going up the hill towards the stones, pulling the Captain's body along the ground. The boy knew that behind the Devil's Door there was a deep hole, covered by long grass and other plants. The Duke made his way slowly to the shadows behind the stones, and when he came out, he was pulling nothing behind him.

'Now for the second!' the boy heard him say. This time the Duke waited outside the hut. It was clear that he expected his wife, the Duchess, to arrive next at the meeting-place.

Inside the hut young Bill shook with fear. 'What will he do if she comes?' he thought. 'Will he kill her too? He looks angry enough! And he can do what he likes – he's the Duke. Nobody can stop him!'

The jealous watcher waited for some time, but she never

came. Sometimes he looked at his watch in surprise. He seemed almost disappointed that she did not appear. At half-past eleven he turned away to find his horse, and rode slowly down the hill.

The young boy thought of what lay in the hole behind the stones, and was too frightened to stay alone in the hut. He preferred to be with someone who was alive, even the

He saw the Duke pulling the Captain's body along the ground.

Duke, than with someone who was dead, so he ran after the horseman. He followed the Duke all the way down into the valley, feeling more comfortable when the lonely hills were left behind him. Soon he could see the high walls and roofs of the Duke's home, Shakeforest Towers.

When the Duke got close to the great house, a small door in a side wall opened, and a woman came out. She ran into the moonlight to meet the Duke.

'Ah, my dear, is it you?' she said. 'I heard your horse's step on the road, and knew it must be you.'

'Happy to see me, are you?'

'How can you ask that?'

'Well, it is a lovely night for meetings.'

'Yes, it is a lovely night.'

The Duke got down from his horse and stood by her side. 'Why were you listening for me at this time of night?' he asked.

'There is a strange story, which I must tell you at once. But why did you come a night sooner than you said? I am sorry, I really am!' (shaking her head playfully), 'because I had ordered a special dinner for your arrival tomorrow, and now it won't be a surprise at all.'

The Duke did not look at his wife. 'What is this strange story that you wish to tell me?' he asked quietly.

'It is this. You know my cousin Fred Ogbourne? We used to play together when we were children, and he – well, he loved me, I think. I told you about it, you know.'

'You have never told me of it before.'

'Ah, my dear, is it you?' the woman said.

'Oh, then it was your sister – yes, I told *her* about it. Well, I haven't seen him for many years, and of course I'd forgotten all about his feeling for me. So I was surprised to receive a letter from him yesterday. I can remember what he wrote.

'*My dear cousin Harriet,* the letter said. *If my life and future mean anything to you at all, I beg you to do what I ask. Meet me at eleven o'clock tonight by the ancient stones on Marlbury Downs. I cannot say more, except to beg you to come. I will explain everything when I see you. Come alone. You have all my happiness in your hands. Yours, Fred*

'That was his letter. *Now* I realize that it was a mistake to go, but at the time I only thought he must be in trouble, and with not a friend in the world to help him. So I went to Marlbury Downs at eleven o'clock. Wasn't it brave of me?'

'Very,' replied the Duke coldly.

'When I got there, I saw he was no longer the boy that I remembered, but a full-grown man and an officer. I was sorry I had come. What he wanted, I don't know – perhaps just a meeting with me. He held me by the hand and waist, and refused to let me go until I promised to meet him again. And in the end I did, because he spoke very warmly to me and I was afraid of him in that lonely place. Then I escaped – I ran home – and that's all. Of course, I never meant to meet him there again. But this evening I thought, "Perhaps he'll come to the house when he realizes I'm not coming to meet him," and that's why I couldn't sleep. But you are so silent!'

'I have had a long journey.'

They moved on towards the front entrance of the house. 'I have thought of something, but perhaps you won't like it,' she said. 'I think he will wait there again tomorrow night. Shall we go to the hill tomorrow together – just to see if he is there? And tell him he must not try to meet me like this?'

'Why should we see if he is there?' asked her unsmiling husband.

'Because I think we should try to help him. Poor Fred! He will listen to you, if you talk to him. It is wrong of him to think of me in that way, but he is clearly very miserable.'

By this time they had reached the front entrance and rung the bell. A man came to take the horse away, and the Duke and Duchess entered the house.

3
Third night

The next night Bill Mills was left alone again to take care of the sheep. He tried bravely not to think of what lay behind the Devil's Door, but without much success. So he was almost pleased as well as surprised when the Duke and Duchess appeared near the hut at about eleven o'clock. He watched and listened through the little window in his hut.

'I tell you, he did not think it was worth coming again!' the Duke said, reluctant to walk further. 'He is not here, so turn round and come home.'

'He doesn't seem to be here, it's true. Perhaps something has happened to him? Oh poor Fred! I do hope he is all right!'

The Duke said quickly, 'Oh, he probably has some other meeting to go to.'

'I don't think so.'

'Or perhaps he has found it too far to come.'

'Nor is that probable.'

'Then perhaps he thought it was better not to come.'

'Yes, perhaps. Or he may be here all the time, hiding behind the Devil's Door. Let's go and see – and surprise him!'

'Oh, he's not there.'

'Perhaps he's lying very quietly in the grass there, because of you,' she said, smiling.

'Oh, no – not because of me!'

'Come, then. Dearest, you're as reluctant as a schoolboy

tonight! I know you're jealous of poor Fred, but you have no reason to be!'

'I'll come! I'll come! Say no more, Harriet!' And together they crossed the grass towards the stones.

The boy came out of the hut to see what happened next, but the Duchess saw him moving in the darkness.

'Ah, I see him at last!' she said.

'See him!' cried the Duke. 'Where?'

'By the Devil's Door. Don't you see him?' She laughed. 'Ah, my poor lover-cousin, you'll be in trouble now!'

'It's not him!' said the Duke in horror. 'It can't be him!'

'No, it isn't. It's too small for him. It's a boy.'

'Ah, I thought so! Boy, come here.'

Fearfully, young Bill came closer.

'What are you doing here?' asked the Duke.

'Taking care of the sheep, your Grace.'

'Ah, you know me! Do you keep sheep here every night?'

'Most nights in winter, your Grace.'

'And what have you seen here tonight or last night?' asked the Duchess. 'Anyone waiting or walking about?'

The boy was silent.

'He has seen nothing,' said her husband quickly, staring angrily at the boy. 'Come, let us go. The air is cold.'

When they had gone, young Bill went back to the sheep. But he was not alone for long. Half an hour later the Duke's heavy steps were heard again. His wife was not with him.

'Listen, boy,' he said. 'The Duchess asked you a question, and I want you to answer it. Have you seen anything strange these nights, when you've been watching your sheep?'

'Your Grace, I'm just a poor, stupid boy, and what I see, I don't remember.'

'I ask you again,' said the Duke, holding the boy's shoulder with a strong hand and staring down into his frightened face. 'Did you see anything strange here last night?'

'Oh, your Grace, don't kill me!' cried the boy, falling to the ground. 'I've never seen you walking here, or riding here, or waiting for a man, or pulling a dead body along!'

'Ah!' said the Duke coldly. 'It is good to know that you have never seen those things. Now, which do you prefer – *to see me do those things now*, or to keep a secret all your life?'

'Keep a secret, your Grace!'

'You are sure you can do it?'

'Oh, try me, your Grace!'

'Very well. And now, do you like being a shepherd?'

'Not at all. 'Tis lonely work for a boy like me, who sees ghosts everywhere. And my master sometimes beats me.'

'I'll give you new clothes, and send you to school, and make a man of you. But you must never say you've been a shepherd boy. The moment that you forget yourself, and speak of what you've seen on the hills – this year, next year, or twenty years from now – I will stop helping you, and you'll come down to being a poor shepherd again.'

'I'll never speak of it, your Grace!'

'Come here.' The Duke took the boy to the Devil's Door. 'Now make a promise in front of these ancient stones. The ghosts that live in this place will find you and punish you if

30

'Oh, your Grace, don't kill me!' cried the boy.

you ever speak of your life as a shepherd boy or what you saw
then. Promise to keep this secret!'

His face as white as a sheet, the boy promised.

Then they went down into the valley, the Duke holding the
boy's hand. That night the boy slept at Shakeforest Towers,
and the next day he was sent away to school.

31

4
Fourth night

On a winter evening many years later, a well-dressed man of business sat in his office at Shakeforest Towers. He had come a long way from the shepherd boy that he once was, but he did not seem happy with his comfortable life. He appeared older than his age, and he looked about him restlessly.

He stood up and left the office, and went to a room in another part of the house, where he knocked, and entered. The Duchess had been dead for some years, and the Duke was now a thin old man with white hair.

'Oh – Mills?' he said. 'Sit down. What is it?'

'Old times have come to life again, your Grace.'

'Which old times are they?'

'That Christmas week twenty-two years ago, when the Duchess's cousin asked her to meet him on Marlbury Downs. I saw the meeting, and I saw much more than that.'

'Do you remember a promise made by a shepherd boy?'

'I do. That boy has kept the promise all his life.'

'Then I wish to hear no more about it.'

'Very well. But the secret may soon come out. Not from me, because I'm grateful for what you've done for me. There was great excitement when Captain Ogbourne disappeared, but I spoke not a word, and his body was never found. For twenty-two years I've wondered what you did with him. Now I know. This afternoon I went up on the hill, and did some digging. I saw enough to know that something still lies there in a hole behind the stones.'

'Mills, do you think the Duchess guessed?'

'She never did, I'm sure, to the day of her death.'

'What made you think of going there this afternoon?'

'Something that happened today, your Grace. The oldest man in the village has died – the old shepherd.'

'Dead at last – how old was he?'

'Ninety-four.'

'And I'm only seventy. I have twenty-four more years!'

'He was my master when I was a shepherd boy, your Grace. And he was on the hill the second night. He was there *all the time*, but none of us knew that.'

'Ah!' said the Duke, looking fixedly at Mills. 'Go on!'

'When I heard he was dying, it made me think of the past, and that's why I went up on the hills. Now the villagers are saying that before he died, he confessed a secret to the vicar – a secret that he'd kept for your Grace, about a crime on Marlbury Downs more than twenty years ago.'

'That's enough, Mills. I'll see the vicar early tomorrow.'

'What will you do, your Grace?'

'Stop his tongue for twenty-four years, until I am dead at ninety-four, like the old shepherd. Go home now, Mills.'

Mills left the room and walked to his own house, where he lived a lonely, friendless life. But he could not sleep, and at midnight he looked out at the colourless moon, and decided to walk up to Marlbury Downs again. Once on the hill, he placed himself where the shepherd's hut had stood. No sheep

*The Duke went to the covered hole, and dug
with his hands like an animal.*

or lambs were there that winter, but the Devil's Door stood high and white as ever, with dark shadows behind it.

Suddenly he realized he was not alone. A figure in white was moving silently towards the stones. It was the Duke himself, in his long nightshirt, walking in his sleep. He went straight to the covered hole, and dug with his hands like an animal. Then he got up, sighed, and went back down the hill. Mills followed him and saw him enter Shakeforest Towers.

The next morning, when Mills arrived at the great house, the housekeeper came to the door to meet him.

'Oh, sir,' she said, 'the Duke is dead! He left his room in the night and went walking around somewhere. And on his way back to his room, he fell downstairs and broke his neck.'

* * *

At last Mills was able to tell the secret that had lain so heavily on his heart for twenty-two years, and he died, at peace with himself, a few years later.

There are still fine sheep and lambs on the Marlbury Downs, but shepherds do not like spending the nights close to the Devil's Door. They say that during Christmas week ghostly white shapes are often seen there. Something made of bright metal shines in the moonlight, and there is the shadow of a man pulling something heavy across the grass. But no one can be sure that these things are true.

A Moment of Madness

1
A wedding is arranged

Most people who knew Baptista Trewthen agreed that there was nothing in her to love, and nothing in her to hate. She did not seem to feel very strongly about anything. But still waters run deep, and nothing had yet happened to make her show what lay hidden inside her, like gold underground.

Since her birth she had lived on St Maria's, an island off the south-west coast of England. Her father, a farmer, had spent a lot of money on sending her to school on the mainland. At nineteen she studied at a training college for teachers, and at twenty-one she found a teaching job in a town called Tor-upon-Sea, on the mainland coast.

Baptista taught the children as well as she could, but after a year had passed she seemed worried about something. Mrs Wace, her landlady, noticed the change in the young woman and asked her what the matter was.

'It has nothing to do with the town, or you,' replied Miss Trewthen. She seemed reluctant to say more.

'Then is it the pay?'

'No, it isn't the pay.'

'Is it something that you've heard from home, my dear?'

Baptista was silent for a few moments. Then she said, 'It's Mr Heddegan–David Heddegan. He's an old neighbour of ours on St Maria's, with no wife or family at all. When I was a child, he used to say he wanted to marry me one day. Now I'm a woman, it's no longer a joke, and he really wishes to do it. And my parents say I can't do better than have him.'

'Has he a lot of money?'

'Yes, he's the richest man that we know.'

'How much older than you is he?'

'Twenty years, maybe more.'

'And is he, perhaps, an unpleasant man?'

'No, he's not unpleasant.'

'Well, child, all I can say is this – don't accept this engagement if it doesn't please you. You're comfortable here in my house, I hope, and I like having you here.'

'Thank you, Mrs Wace. You're very kind to me. But here comes my difficulty. I don't like teaching. Ah, you're surprised. That's because I've hidden it from everyone. Well, I really hate school. The children are awful little things, who make trouble all day long. But even *they* are not as bad as the inspector. For the three months before his visit I woke up several times every night, worrying about it. It's so difficult knowing what to teach and what to leave untaught! I think father and mother are right. They say I'll never be a good teacher if I don't like the work, so I should marry Mr Heddegan and then I won't need to work. I don't know what to do, Mrs Wace. I like him better than teaching, but I don't like him enough to marry him.'

These conversations were continued from day to day, until at last the landlady decided to agree with Baptista's parents.

'Life will be much easier for you, my dear,' she told her young friend, 'if you marry this rich neighbour.'

In April Baptista went home to St Maria's for a short holiday, and when she returned, she seemed calmer.

'I have agreed to have him as my husband, so that's the end of it,' she told Mrs Wace.

In the next few months letters passed between Baptista and Mr Heddegan, but the girl preferred not to discuss her engagement with Mrs Wace. Later, she told her that she was leaving her job at the end of July, and the wedding was arranged for the first Wednesday in August.

2
A chance meeting

When the end of July arrived, Baptista was in no hurry to return home to the island. She was not planning to buy any special clothes for the wedding, and her parents were making all the other arrangements. So she did not leave Tor-upon-Sea until the Saturday before her wedding. She travelled by train to the town of Pen-zephyr, but when she arrived, she found that the boat to St Maria's had left early, and there was no other boat until Tuesday. 'I'll have to stay here until then,' she thought. 'It's too far to go back to Mrs Wace's.' She did not seem to mind this – in fact, she was almost happy to wait another three nights before seeing her future husband.

She found a room in a small hotel, took her luggage there, then went out for a walk round the town.

'Oh, is it really you, Charles?' Baptista said.

'Baptista? Yes, Baptista it is!'

The words came from behind her. Turning round, she gave a jump, and stared. 'Oh, is it really you, Charles?' she said.

With a half-smile the newcomer looked her up and down. He appeared almost angry with her, but he said nothing.

'I'm going home,' she continued, 'but I've missed the boat.'

He did not seem interested in this news. 'Still teaching?' he said. 'What a fine teacher you make, Baptista, I'm sure!'

39

She knew that was not his real meaning. 'I know I'm not very good at teaching,' she replied. 'That's why I've stopped.'

'Oh, you've stopped? You surprise me.'

'I hate teaching.'

'Perhaps that's because *I'm* a teacher.'

'Oh no, it isn't. It's because I'm starting a new life. Next week I'm going to marry Mr David Heddegan.'

At this unexpected reply, the young man took a step back. 'Who is Mr David Heddegan?' he said, trying to sound bored.

'He owns a number of shops on St Maria's, and he's my father's neighbour and oldest friend.'

'So, no longer a schoolteacher, just a shopkeeper's wife. I knew you would never succeed as a teacher. You're like a woman who thinks she can be a great actress just because she has a beautiful face, and forgets she has to be able to act. But you found out your mistake early, didn't you?'

'Don't be unpleasant to me, Charles,' Baptista said sadly.

'I'm not being unpleasant – I'm just saying what is true, in a friendly way – although I do have good reason to be unpleasant to you. What a hurry you've been in, Baptista! I do hate a woman in a hurry!'

'What do you mean?'

'Well – in a hurry to be somebody's wife. Any husband is better than no husband for you, it seems. You couldn't wait for me, oh no! Well, thank God, that's all in the past for me!'

'Wait for you? What does that mean, Charley? You never showed that you felt anything special for me.'

'Oh really, Baptista dear!'

'What I mean is, there was nothing that I could be sure of. I suppose you liked me a little, but I didn't think you meant to make an honest engagement of it.'

'That's just it! You girls expect a man to talk about marrying after the first look! But I *did* mean to get engaged to you, you know.'

'But you never said so, and a woman can't wait for ever!'

'Baptista, I promise you that I was planning to ask you to marry me in six months' time.'

She appeared very uncomfortable, and they walked along in silence. Soon he said, 'Did you want to marry me then?'

And she whispered sadly back, 'Yes!'

As they walked on, away from the town and into the fields, her shoulder and his were close together. He held her arm with a strong hand. This seemed to say, 'Now I hold you, and you must do what I want.'

'How strange that we should meet like this!' said the young man. 'You and I could be husband and wife, going on our honeymoon together. But instead of that, we'll say goodbye in half an hour, perhaps for ever. Yes, life is strange!'

She stopped walking. 'I must go back. This is too painful, Charley! You're not being kind today.'

'I don't want to hurt you – you know I don't,' he answered more gently. 'But it makes me angry – what you're going to do. I don't think you should marry him.'

'I must do it, now that I've agreed.'

'Why?' he asked, speaking more seriously now. 'It's never too late to stop a wedding if you're not happy with it. Now

41

– you could marry me, instead of him, although you were in too much of a hurry to wait for me!'

'Oh, it isn't possible to think of that!' she cried, shaking her head. 'At home everything will be ready for the wedding!'

'If we marry, it must be at once. This evening you can come back with me to Trufal, the town where I live. We can get married there on Tuesday, and then no Mr David Heddegan, or anyone else, can take you away from me!'

'But I must go home on the Tuesday boat,' she said worriedly. 'What will they think if I don't arrive?'

'You can go home on that boat just the same. The only difference is that I'll go with you. You'll tell your parents that you've married a young man with a good job, someone that you met at the training college. When I meet them, they'll accept that we're married and it can't be changed. And you won't be miserable for ever as the wife of an awful old man. Now honestly, you do like me best, don't you, Baptista?'

'Yes,' she whispered.

'Then we will do what I say.'

3
Baptista gets married

That same afternoon Charles Stow and Baptista Trewthen travelled by train to the town of Trufal. Charles was, surprisingly, very careful of appearances, and found a room for Baptista in a different house from where he was staying.

'You could marry me, instead of him,' said Charles.

On Sunday they went to church and then walked around the town, on Monday Charles made the arrangements, and by nine o'clock on Tuesday morning they were husband and wife.

For the first time in her life Baptista had gone against her parents' wishes. She went cold with fear when she thought of their first meeting with her new husband. But she felt she had to tell them as soon as possible, and now the most important thing was to get home to St Maria's. So, in a great hurry, they packed their bags and caught the train to Pen-zephyr.

They arrived two hours before the boat left, so to pass the time they decided to walk along the cliffs a little way. It was a hot summer day, and Charles wanted to have a swim in the sea. Baptista did not like the idea of sitting alone while he swam. 'But I'll only be a quarter of an hour,' Charles said, and Baptista passively accepted this.

She sat high up on the cliffs, and watched him go down a footpath, disappear, appear again, and run across the beach to the sea. She watched him for a moment, then stared out to sea, thinking about her family. They were probably not worried about her, because she had sometimes missed the boat before, but they were expecting her to arrive today – and to marry David Heddegan tomorrow. 'How angry father will be!' she thought miserably. 'And mother will say I've made a terrible mistake! I almost wish I hadn't married Charles, in that moment of madness! Oh dear, what have I done!'

This made her think of her new husband, and she turned to look for him. He did not appear to be in the sea any more, and she could not see him on the beach. By this time she was frightened, and she climbed down the path as quickly as her shaking legs could manage. On the beach she called two men to help her, but they said they could see nothing at all in the water. Soon she found the place where Charles had left his clothes, but by now the sea had carried them away.

For a few minutes she stood there without moving. There was only one way to explain this sudden disappearance – her husband had drowned. And as she stood there, it began to seem like a terrible dream, and the last three days of her life with Charles seemed to disappear. She even had difficulty in remembering his face. 'How unexpected it was, meeting him that day!' she thought. 'And the wedding – did I really agree to it? Are we really married? It all happened so fast!'

She began to cry, still standing there on the beach. She did not know what to do, or even what to think. Finally, she remembered the boat, and catching the boat home seemed the easiest thing to do. So she walked to the station, arranged for someone to carry her luggage, and went down to the boat. She did all this automatically, in a kind of dream.

Just before the boat left, she heard part of a conversation which made her sure that Charles was dead. One passenger said to another, 'A man drowned here earlier today, you know. He swam out too far, they say. A stranger, I think. Some people in a boat saw him, but they couldn't get to him in time.'

The boat was a long way out to sea before Baptista realized that Mr Heddegan was on the boat with her. She saw him

As Baptista stood there, it began to seem like a terrible dream.

walking towards her and quickly took the wedding ring off her left hand.

'I hope you're well, my dear?' he said. He was a healthy, red-faced man of fifty-five. 'I wanted to come across to meet you. What bad luck that you missed the boat on Saturday!'

46

And Baptista had to agree, and smile, and make conversation. Mr Heddegan had spoken to her before she was ready to say anything. Now the moment had passed.

When the boat arrived, her parents were there to meet her. Her father walked home beside Mr Heddegan, while her mother walked next to Baptista, talking all the time.

'I'm so happy, my child,' said Mrs Trewthen in her loud, cheerful voice, 'that you've kept your promise to marry Mr Heddegan. How busy we've been! But now things are all ready for the wedding, and a few friends and neighbours are coming in for supper this evening.' Again, the moment for confessing had passed, and Baptista stayed silent.

When they reached home, Mrs Trewthen said, 'Now, Baptista, hurry up to your room and take off your hat, then come downstairs. I must go to the kitchen.'

The young woman passively obeyed her mother's orders. The evening was a great success for all except Baptista. She had no chance to tell her parents the news, and it was already much more difficult than it had been at first. By the end of the evening, when all the neighbours had left, she found herself alone in her bedroom again. She had come home with much to say, and had said none of it. She now realized that she was not brave enough to tell her story. And as the clock struck midnight, she decided it should stay untold.

Morning came, and when she thought of Charles, it was more with fear than with love. Her mother called from downstairs, 'Baptista! Time to get up! Mr Heddegan will be at the church in three-quarters of an hour!'

Baptista got out of bed, looked out of the window, and took the easy way. She put her best clothes on, confessed nothing, and kept her promise to marry David Heddegan.

4
The honeymoon

Mr Heddegan did not worry about his new wife's coldness towards him during and after the wedding. 'I know she was reluctant to marry me,' he thought, 'but that will pass. Things'll be different in a few months' time!'

During the wedding dinner, someone asked Heddegan about the honeymoon. To Baptista's horror, he answered, 'Oh, we're going to spend a few days in Pen-zephyr.'

'What!' cried Baptista. 'I know nothing of this!'

Because of her late arrival, Heddegan had not been able to ask where *she* would like to spend the honeymoon, so he had arranged a trip to the mainland. It was difficult to change these plans at the last minute, so she had to agree, and that evening she and her new husband arrived in Pen-zephyr.

Their first problem was finding a hotel, because the fine weather had filled the town with tourists. They walked from place to place, Heddegan polite and friendly, Baptista cold and silent. Finally they found an excellent hotel, which to their surprise was empty. Kindly Mr Heddegan, who wanted to please his young wife, asked for the best room on the first floor, with a good view of the sea.

'I'm sorry,' said the landlady, 'there's a gentleman in that room.' Then, seeing Heddegan's disappointed face, and not wishing to lose a customer, she added quickly, 'But perhaps the gentleman will agree to move to another room, and then you can have the one that you want.'

'Well, if he doesn't want a view . . .' said Mr Heddegan.

'Oh no, I'm sure he doesn't. And if you don't mind going for a little walk, I'll have the room ready when you return.'

During their walk, Baptista was careful to choose different streets from those that she had walked down with Charles, and her white face showed how difficult this visit was for her. At last they returned to the hotel, and were shown into the best bedroom. They sat at the window, drinking tea. Although Heddegan had arranged for a sea view, to please Baptista, she did not look out of the window once, but kept her eyes on the floor and walls of the room.

Suddenly she noticed a hat on the back of the door. It was just like the hat that Charles had worn. She stared harder; yes, it was the actual hat! She fell back in her chair.

Her husband jumped up, saying worriedly, 'You're not well! What can I get ye?'

'Smelling salts!' she said quickly, her voice shaking a little. 'From the shop near the station!'

He ran out of the room. Baptista rang the bell, and when a young girl came, whispered to her, 'That hat! Whose is it?'

'Oh, I'm sorry, I'll take it away,' said the girl hurriedly. She took the hat off the door. 'It belongs to the other gentleman.'

'Where is – the other gentleman?' asked Baptista.

'He's in the next room, madam. He *was* in here.'

'But I can't hear him! I don't think he's there.'

'He makes no noise, but he's there,' replied the girl.

Suddenly Baptista understood what the girl meant, and a cold hand lay on her heart.

'Why is he so silent?' she whispered.

'If I tell you, please don't say anything to the landlady,' begged the girl, 'or I'll lose my job! It's because he's dead. He's

'He makes no noise, but he's there,' said the girl.

50

the young teacher who drowned yesterday. They brought his body here, and that's why there's nobody staying in the hotel. People don't like a dead body in the house. But we've changed the sheets and cleaned the room, madam!'

Just then Heddegan arrived with the smelling salts, and the girl left the room. 'Any better?' he asked Baptista.

'I don't like the hotel!' she cried. 'We'll have to leave!'

For the first time Heddegan spoke crossly to his wife. 'Now that's enough, Baptista! First you want one thing, then another! It's cost me enough, in money and words, to get this fine room, and it's too much to expect me to find another hotel at this time of the evening. We'll stay quietly here tonight, do ye hear? And find another place tomorrow.'

The young woman said no more. Her mind was cold with horror. That night she lay between the two men who she had married, David Heddegan on one side, and, on the other side through the bedroom wall, Charles Stow.

5
Secrets discovered

Mr and Mrs Heddegan both felt the honeymoon was not a success. They were happy to return to the island and start married life together in David Heddegan's large house. Baptista soon became as calm and passive as she had been before. She even smiled when neighbours called her Mrs Heddegan, and she began to enjoy the comfortable life that a rich husband could offer her. She did nothing at all to stop people finding out about her first marriage to Charles Stow, although there was always a danger of that happening.

One evening in September, when she was standing in her garden, a workman walked past along the road. He seemed to recognize her, and spoke to her in friendly surprise.

'What! Don't you know me?' he asked.

'I'm afraid I don't,' said Baptista.

'I was your witness, madam. I was mending the church window when you and your young man came to get married. Don't you remember? The vicar called me, to be a witness.'

Baptista looked quickly around. Heddegan was at the other end of the garden but unluckily, just at that moment, he turned and walked towards the house. 'Are you coming in, my dear?' he called out to Baptista.

The workman stared at him. 'That's not your—' he began, then he saw Baptista's face and stopped. Baptista was unable to speak, and the workman began to realize that there was a little mystery here. 'I've been unlucky since then,' he continued, still staring at Baptista's white face. 'It's hard finding enough work to buy food for my wife and myself. Perhaps you could help me, because I once helped you?'

Baptista gave him some money, and hoped never to see him again. But he was cleverer than he looked. By asking questions on the island and the mainland, he soon realized that Baptista had married one man on Tuesday, and another man on Wednesday. He visited her again two days later.

'It was a mystery to me, madam!' he said, when she opened the door. 'But now I understand it all. I want to tell you,

The workman began to realize that there was a little mystery here.

madam, that I'm not a man to make trouble between husband and wife. But I'm going back to the mainland again, and I need a little more money. If your old man finds out about your first husband, I'm sure he won't like it, will he?'

She knew he was right, and paid him what he wanted. A week later the workman sent his wife to ask for more money, and again Baptista paid. But when there was a fourth visit, she refused to pay, and shut the door in the man's surprised face.

She knew she had to tell her husband everything. She liked him better now than she had done at first, and did not want to lose him, but her secret was no longer safe. She went to find him, and said, 'David, I have something to tell you.'

'Yes, my dear,' he said with a sigh. In the last week he had been less cheerful and had seemed worried about something.

When they were both in the sitting room, she said, 'David, perhaps you will hate me for this, but I must confess something that I've hidden from you. It happened before we were married. And it's about a lover.'

'I don't mind. In fact, I was hoping it was more than that.'

'Well, it was. I met my old lover by chance, and he asked me, and – well, I married him. We were coming here to tell you, but he drowned, and I said nothing about him, and then I married you, David, for peace and quietness. Now you'll be angry with me, I know you will!'

She spoke wildly, and expected her husband to shout and scream. But instead, the old man jumped up and began to dance happily around the room.

'Oh, wonderful!' he cried. 'How lucky! My dear Baptista, I see a way out of my difficulty – ha-ha!'

'What do you mean?' she asked, afraid he had gone mad.

'Oh my dear, *I've* got something to confess too! You see, I was friendly with a woman in Pen-zephyr for many years – *very* friendly, you could say – and in the end I married her just before she died. I kept it secret, but people here are beginning to talk. And I've got four big girls to think of—'

'Oh David, four daughters!' she cried in horror.

'*And I've got four big girls to think of—*'

'That's right, my dear. I'm sorry to say they haven't been to school at all. I'd like to bring them to live here with us, and I thought, by marrying a teacher, I could get someone to teach them, all for nothing. What do you think, Baptista?'

'Four grown girls, always around the house! And I hate teaching, it kills me! But I must do it, I can see that. I am punished for that moment of madness, I really am!'

Here the conversation ended. The next day Baptista had to welcome her husband's daughters into her home. They were not good-looking or intelligent or even well-dressed, and poor Baptista could only look forward to years of hard work with them. She went about, sighing miserably, with no hope for the future.

But when Heddegan asked her a month later, 'How do you like 'em now?' her answer was unexpected.

'Much better than at first,' she said. 'I may like them very much one day.'

And so began a more pleasant time for Baptista Heddegan. She had discovered what kind, gentle girls these unwelcome daughters were. At first she felt sorry for them, then grew to like them. And from liking, she grew to love them. In the end they brought her and her husband closer together, and so Baptista and David were able to put the past behind them and find unexpected happiness in their married life.

GLOSSARY

ancient very old

appearance what someone or something looks like or seems

arrange to make a plan for the future

arrangement a plan or preparation for a future event

beg to ask somebody for something in a very strong way

birth when a child is born

cheerful looking or sounding happy

cliff the high steep side of a hill by the sea

confess to tell the truth about something you have done wrong

cottage a small house, usually in the country

cousin the son or daughter of your uncle or aunt

Devil the opposite of God

disappointed sad because what you wanted did not happen

dishonour to make somebody lose the respect of other people

drown to die in water because you cannot breathe

Duchess the wife of a Duke

Duke a title for a man of the highest social position

engaged when you have promised to marry someone

engagement an agreement to marry

expect to think or believe that something will happen

fiddler a person who plays a fiddle (a violin)

footpath a path for people to walk on, usually in the country

gentleman a man of good family, usually rich

grave a hole in the ground where a dead person is buried

hang to kill someone by letting them drop from a tree or a
wooden post, with a rope around their neck

hangman a person whose job is to hang criminals

honey a sweet sticky food that is made by bees

honeymoon a holiday for a man and a woman who have just
  got married
horror a feeling of great fear or shock
hut a very small, simple building, often made of wood
jealous angry or sad because someone you love is showing
  interest in another person
joke something that you say or do to make people laugh
judge the person in a lawcourt who decides how to punish
  someone
lamb a young sheep
landlady a woman who owns a house where other people pay to
  live
madness crazy or stupid behaviour
mainland the main part of a country, not the islands around it
master *(old-fashioned)* a man who has people working for him
mead a sweet alcoholic drink made from honey and eggs
mug a large cup with straight sides and a handle
passive *(adj)* accepting what happens or what people do without
  trying to change anything
reluctant not wanting to do something
rope very thick strong string
shepherd a man who takes care of sheep
sigh to breathe out once very deeply, when you are sad or tired
smelling salts a chemical with a very strong smell, kept in a
  small bottle, used in the past for putting under the nose of a
  person who feels faint
stove a heater
strike (past tense **struck**) of a clock, to tell the time by sounding
  a bell
training college (in this story) a place where people study to
  become teachers

tobacco   what people smoke in cigarettes and pipes
vicar   a priest in the Church of England
view   what you can see from a particular place
waist   the part around the middle of your body
witness   at a wedding, someone who writes their name in the church register to prove they saw the marriage happen
your Grace   words you say when speaking to a Duke or Duchess

WESSEX DIALECT WORDS USED IN THE STORY

'tis   it is
ye   you
'em   them
o'   of

Before Reading

1 Read the introduction on the first page of the book, and the back cover. Who or what do you think you will find in these stories? Look at the story titles and choose from these lists.

The Three Strangers   *What the Shepherd Saw*
A Moment of Madness

a duke	a school	sheep
a ghost	a party	horses
a pilot	a honeymoon	secret meetings
a jealous husband	a car chase	emails
a prisoner	a death	chickens
a mad person	a murder	lambs

2 What can you guess about these stories? Choose endings for these sentences. (You can choose more than one if you like.)

The Three Strangers

1 The first stranger comes to the cottage because . . .

a) he is running away from something.

b) he wants to dry his clothes.

c) he is looking for somebody.

2 The second stranger comes to the cottage because . . .

a) he is running away from something.

b) he wants to dry his clothes.

c) he is looking for somebody.

What the Shepherd Saw

3 The young shepherd boy sees a secret meeting between . . .

  a) a woman and her brother.

  b) a woman and her lover.

  c) a woman and her cousin.

4 The next night there is a meeting between . . .

  a) the same woman and the same man.

  b) the same man and the woman's husband.

  c) the same woman and her husband.

A Moment of Madness

5 The teacher is going to marry an older man . . .

  a) to please her parents.

  b) to please herself.

  c) to escape from her job as a teacher.

6 At the end of this story the teacher . . .

  a) is married to a different man.

  b) is married to the older man.

  c) is married to her second husband.

3 **Before you read the first story, *The Three Strangers*, what do you think is going to happen? Answer each question with Y (yes), N (no) or P (perhaps).**

  1 Will the first stranger leave the cottage in a hurry when the second stranger arrives? Y/N/P

  2 Will someone die before the end of the story? Y/N/P

  3 Will the story end happily? Y/N/P

While Reading

Read *The Three Strangers,* to the end of page 12. Who said this, and to whom? Who or what were they talking about?

1 'There's only one more thing that I need to make me happy.'
2 'Oh, but you can't stop making this!'
3 'He hasn't gone far, I'm sure.'
4 'We'll save ourselves all that trouble.'

Before you finish reading *The Three Strangers*, can you guess the answers to these questions? Choose from these ideas (you can choose more than one).

1 Who is the third stranger?
   a) The escaped prisoner   d) The prisoner's brother
   b) A madman   e) A man with a terrible secret
   c) A clockmaker   f) A man who has seen a ghost
2 What do you think will happen at the end of the story?
   a) The prison officers will catch the escaped prisoner.
   b) The hangman will do his work at the prison tomorrow.
   c) The shepherd and his friends will go to prison because they let the clockmaker escape.
   d) The clockmaker will escape, and no one will ever see him again.

Read *What the Shepherd Saw*, to the end of page 31. Before you finish the story, can you guess what happens? Choose T (true) or F (false) for each of these ideas.

1 Bill Mills keeps his promise, and while the Duke is alive, he never tells anyone about Fred Ogbourne's murder. T/F
2 The Duke kills the boy, to stop him telling the truth. T/F
3 The Duchess discovers the murder, and leaves the Duke. T/F
4 The Duke confesses, and is sent to prison. T/F
5 Another person who saw the murder talks about it. T/F
6 Mills has a happy life at Shakeforest Towers. T/F
7 The true story only comes out after the Duke's death. T/F

Read *A Moment of Madness*, to the end of page 53. Before you finish the story, can you guess what happens next? Choose some of these ideas.

Baptista . . .
1 tells her husband everything.
2 does nothing, hoping that the workman will lose interest.
3 arranges to pay the workman some money every month.
4 asks her mother what she should do.
If David Heddegan learns the truth, he will . . .
5 be angry, and send Baptista back to her family.
6 be happy, because he has a secret of his own to confess.
7 be disappointed with Baptista, because she was not honest with him.
8 do something which Baptista feels is a punishment.

After Reading

1 **Perhaps this is what some of the characters in the stories were thinking. Which characters are they (two from each story), and what has just happened in the story?**

   1 'Is that really her walking down the street? The farmer's daughter who seemed so sure she'd be a good teacher! She's prettier than ever – I wonder if she still likes me?'

   2 'Now, I'll go up to the hut very quietly through the trees and see if that boy o' mine is asleep inside. Wait – who's this? The Duke! What's he doing up here? Oh no, no!'

   3 'What *am* I going to do? There's Jeb, and the man next to him is saying he's the hangman! I *mustn't* show that I recognize Jeb . . . I'll have to run away – *now*!'

   4 'That's his horse on the road, I know it is. He's come home a day early. I'll run down at once and tell him about Fred. Then he can't be jealous if Fred comes to the house.'

   5 'Well, here's a mystery! What happened to the young man she married when I was a witness? Perhaps I can make some money out of this. I'll be back, lady, I'll be back!'

   6 'I'll walk all night now, after that cake and mead. My poor brother – his face was so white! Good thing he ran away – they'll be busy chasing him for a while, and I can get away.'

2 A prison officer is talking to the hangman, the day after the strangers visited the cottage. Put their conversation in the right order, and write in who the speakers are. The officer speaks first (number 2).

1 _____ 'But that's my man, surely!'

2 _____ 'I'm sorry, you'll have no work to do this morning.'

3 _____ 'Yes, you have! You were sitting next to him!'

4 _____ 'Yes. The man in the chimney corner drinking mead with you and smoking his pipe – he was our prisoner!'

5 _____ 'Why's that then? Didn't the men at the cottage catch the escaped prisoner last night?'

6 _____ 'No, he's the prisoner's brother. He was on his way to make his last visit to him in Casterbridge prison.'

7 _____ 'What! You don't mean to say—'

8 _____ 'No, they only caught a little man with fair hair.'

9 _____ 'So where's the prisoner himself then? Hasn't anybody seen him since he escaped?'

3 Here are some different titles for the stories. Which ones are suitable for which stories? Explain why. Which titles do you prefer? Can you think of any more?

- The Hangman's Visit
- An Honest Wife
- Death by Drowning
- Mead and Mystery
- Honeymoon of Horror
- Footpath to Freedom
- The Devil's Door
- A Wanted Man
- The Wedding Witness
- Meetings by Moonlight
- A Hidden Grave
- The Two Husbands

4 **Here is Baptista telling her mother about David Heddegan's secret. Complete Baptista's part of the conversation.**

MOTHER: You look worried, dear. Is anything the matter?
BAPTISTA: _____
MOTHER: Really? What kind of secret?
BAPTISTA: _____
MOTHER: He *married* her? Well, she's dead now, dear, and at least there are no children to worry about!
BAPTISTA: _____
MOTHER: What! Four daughters! And what's he going to do with them?
BAPTISTA: _____
MOTHER: Oh no! He can't do this to you, Baptista, and we must stop him!

5 **At the end of the conversation above, there are two ways that Baptista could reply to her mother. She could confess her own secret, or she could say nothing about it and pretend she doesn't mind. Write the two different replies below.**

1 BAPTISTA: We can't stop him, because _____
2 BAPTISTA: No, don't say anything. Perhaps _____

6 **What did you think about the secrets in this story? Do you agree or disagree with these statements? Explain why.**

1 David's secret was much worse than Baptista's.
2 It is always better to tell the truth.
3 There are times when the truth is not necessary.

7 **After the Duke died, Bill Mills was able to talk about his secret at last. Complete what he says with the linking words below. (Use each one once.)**

after / although / and / and / because / but / but / if / so / that / to / until / what / what / when / where / who

It all happened up at the Devil's Door. Captain Ogbourne, _____ was the Duchess's cousin, came to meet her there. I was looking out of the window of the hut, _____ I could see everything. He had come _____ tell her he loved her, and, _____ she didn't say she still loved him, she agreed to meet him the next night. _____ they'd gone, the Duke appeared from behind the stones. I realize now _____ he thought they were lovers, _____ he was too far away to hear _____ they were saying. The next night he arrived early, _____ waited in the hut _____ I was hiding. _____ the Captain arrived, the Duke went out and killed him. _____ you look in that hole behind the Devil's Door, you'll find _____'s left of his dead body. I know it was wrong to keep it a secret all these years, _____ I was only a boy then. The Duke made me promise to stay silent _____ I kept that promise _____ he died, _____, like everybody else, I've always been afraid of him.

8 **Which of these characters did you like, or dislike? Which did you feel sorry for? Give your reasons.**

- The clockmaker / His brother / The hangman
- Bill Mills / The Duke / The Duchess / Fred Ogbourne
- Baptista / Charles Stow / David Heddegan

ABOUT THE AUTHOR

Thomas Hardy (1840–1928) was born in the village of Higher Bockhampton in Dorset, in the south of England. While he was a young man, he often played the fiddle at weddings and parties, and he used to love listening to old people telling stories of country life. Were the stories true? Hardy once described one of the old musicians from his village as 'a man who speaks neither truth or lies, but something halfway between the two which is very enjoyable'. Later in his life, Hardy put many of the characters and events from these old tales into his own short stories and novels.

At twenty-two he went to London to work as an architect, and there he started writing poems and stories and novels. His fourth novel, *Far from the Madding Crowd* (1874), was very popular, and from this he earned enough money to stop working and also to get married. Other successful novels followed, but when *Tess of the d'Urbervilles* (1891) and *Jude the Obscure* (1895) were published, readers did not like them at all, saying they were dark and cruel. After this, Hardy stopped writing novels and returned to poetry.

For most of his life he lived in Dorset with his first wife Emma, and soon after she died he married again. After his death his heart was buried in Emma's grave.

The Three Strangers, one of Hardy's best known short stories, comes from a volume called *Wessex Tales*, and *What the Shepherd Saw* and *A Moment of Madness* (the original title was *A Mere Interlude*) come from a volume called *A Changed Man and Other Tales*.

OXFORD BOOKWORMS LIBRARY

Classics • Crime & Mystery • Factfiles • Fantasy & Horror
Human Interest • Playscripts • Thriller & Adventure
True Stories • World Stories

The OXFORD BOOKWORMS LIBRARY provides enjoyable reading in English, with a wide range of classic and modern fiction, non-fiction, and plays. It includes original and adapted texts in seven carefully graded language stages, which take learners from beginner to advanced level. An overview is given on the next pages.

All Stage 1 titles are available as audio recordings, as well as over eighty other titles from Starter to Stage 6. All Starters and many titles at Stages 1 to 4 are specially recommended for younger learners. Every Bookworm is illustrated, and Starters and Factfiles have full-colour illustrations.

The OXFORD BOOKWORMS LIBRARY also offers extensive support. Each book contains an introduction to the story, notes about the author, a glossary, and activities. Additional resources include tests and worksheets, and answers for these and for the activities in the books. There is advice on running a class library, using audio recordings, and the many ways of using Oxford Bookworms in reading programmes. Resource materials are available on the website <www.oup.com/bookworms>.

The *Oxford Bookworms Collection* is a series for advanced learners. It consists of volumes of short stories by well-known authors, both classic and modern. Texts are not abridged or adapted in any way, but carefully selected to be accessible to the advanced student.

You can find details and a full list of titles in the *Oxford Bookworms Library Catalogue* and *Oxford English Language Teaching Catalogues*, and on the website <www.oup.com/bookworms>.

THE OXFORD BOOKWORMS LIBRARY
GRADING AND SAMPLE EXTRACTS

STARTER • 250 HEADWORDS

present simple – present continuous – imperative –
can/cannot, must – *going to* (future) – simple gerunds …

Her phone is ringing – but where is it?

Sally gets out of bed and looks in her bag. No phone. She looks under the bed. No phone. Then she looks behind the door. There is her phone. Sally picks up her phone and answers it. *Sally's Phone*

STAGE 1 • 400 HEADWORDS

… past simple – coordination with *and*, *but*, *or* –
subordination with *before*, *after*, *when*, *because*, *so* …

I knew him in Persia. He was a famous builder and I worked with him there. For a time I was his friend, but not for long. When he came to Paris, I came after him – I wanted to watch him. He was a very clever, very dangerous man. *The Phantom of the Opera*

STAGE 2 • 700 HEADWORDS

… present perfect – *will* (future) – *(don't) have to, must not, could* –
comparison of adjectives – simple *if* clauses – past continuous –
tag questions – *ask/tell* + infinitive …

While I was writing these words in my diary, I decided what to do. I must try to escape. I shall try to get down the wall outside. The window is high above the ground, but I have to try. I shall take some of the gold with me – if I escape, perhaps it will be helpful later. *Dracula*

... should, may – present perfect continuous – *used to* – past perfect –
causative – relative clauses – indirect statements ...

Of course, it was most important that no one should see
Colin, Mary, or Dickon entering the secret garden. So Colin
gave orders to the gardeners that they must all keep away
from that part of the garden in future. ***The Secret Garden***

... past perfect continuous – passive (simple forms) –
would conditional clauses – indirect questions –
relatives with *where/when* – gerunds after prepositions/phrases ...

I was glad. Now Hyde could not show his face to the world
again. If he did, every honest man in London would be proud
to report him to the police. ***Dr Jekyll and Mr Hyde***

... future continuous – future perfect –
passive (modals, continuous forms) –
would have conditional clauses – modals + perfect infinitive ...

If he had spoken Estella's name, I would have hit him. I was so
angry with him, and so depressed about my future, that I could
not eat the breakfast. Instead I went straight to the old house.
Great Expectations

... passive (infinitives, gerunds) – advanced modal meanings –
clauses of concession, condition

When I stepped up to the piano, I was confident. It was as if I
knew that the prodigy side of me really did exist. And when I
started to play, I was so caught up in how lovely I looked that
I didn't worry how I would sound. ***The Joy Luck Club***

BOOKWORMS · CLASSICS · STAGE 3

A Christmas Carol

CHARLES DICKENS

Retold by Clare West

Christmas is humbug, Scrooge says – just a time when you find yourself a year older and not a penny richer. The only thing that matters to Scrooge is business, and making money.

But on Christmas Eve three spirits come to visit him. They take him travelling on the wings of the night to see the shadows of Christmas past, present, and future – and Scrooge learns a lesson that he will never forget.

BOOKWORMS · TRUE STORIES · STAGE 3

Rabbit-Proof Fence

DORIS PILKINGTON GARIMARA

Retold by Jennifer Bassett

Fourteen-year-old Molly and her cousins Daisy and Gracie were mixed-race Aborigines. In 1931 they were taken away from their families and sent to a camp to be trained as good 'white' Australians. They were told to forget their mothers, their language, their home.

But Molly would not forget. She and her cousins escaped and walked back to Jigalong, 1600 kilometres away, following the rabbit-proof fence north across Western Australia to their desert home.

Rabbit-Proof Fence is the true story of that walk, told by Molly's daughter, Doris. It is also a prize-winning film.